Hey God

Why Is Life So Hard?

An Atheist asks, God answers

Kya Rose

Hey God, Why Is Life So Hard?

An Atheist asks,
God answers

by
Kya Rose

❧ Copyright © 2020 Kya Rose ☙

Copyright © 2020 Kya Rose

All Rights Reserved.

ISBN: 978-1-7348570-0-9 Paperback edition

ISBN: 978-1-7348570-1-6 Ebook edition

Cover/ title page photo credit to NASA, design by Kya Rose.

No part of this book may be used or reproduced by any means, graphic, electronic, or mechanical, including photocopying, recording, taping, or by any information storage retrieval system without the written permission of the author except in the case of brief quotations embodied in articles and reviews.

This book is not intended as a substitute for medical advice. Readers are encouraged to consult their physician in matters relating to their health, particularly with respect to any symptoms that may require diagnosis or medical attention.

Although the author has made every effort to ensure that the information in this book was correct at press time, the author does not assume and hereby disclaims any liability to any party for any loss, damage, or disruption caused by errors or omissions, whether such errors or omissions result from negligence, accident, or any other cause.

For more information, please visit: www.MagickLessons.com

Wise Peacock
Publications
Lansing, MI

Table of contents

Preface

Chapter One - Hey God 1
    God the Infinite 2
    God the Personal 4
    God the King 6

Chapter Two - Why Is Life So Hard? . . 11
    Unresolved Childhood Emotions 11
    Global Economic Deception 14
    Authoritarian Governance 15
    Energetic Depression 16
    Limiting Ideas About Divinity 18
    We Forgot That We Are Magical 19
    Proposal For Humanity 21

Chapter Three - An Atheist Asks 23
    Books Don't Have Answers 23
    Soup 24
    Communication 25
    Speaking . , ... 27

Listening 29
Our Inner Dialogue 30
The Placebo Effect 32

Chapter Four - God Answers 35
Merely Sprouts 36
Our Inner Prism 37

Chapter Five - Magick Lessons 41
Light Work 42
Simple Light Work Tools . 43
Shadow Work 46

Chapter Six - Exercises 48
Exercise One
   Inhale Magick, Exhale Magick 50
Exercise Two
   Magick Above, Magick Below 52
Exercise Three
   Divine Dance Party 55
Exercise Four
   Appreciation 59

Exercise Five
> **How Great Would That Be?** 61

Exercise Six
> **Building Affirmations 2.0** 63

Exercise Seven
> **Magick "To Do" Lists** 68

Exercise Eight
> **Back From The Future Meditation** . . 70

Exercise Nine
> **Temple of Mind Meditation** 72

Exercise Ten
> **Shadow Work Process** 77

Pleasure Maps 88
Appreciation Journal 96

Kya's Story *100*
Notes *104*
About the Author *106*

⊰ Dedications ⊱

Thank you

To Faerin,
For 23 amazing years

To Rowan,
 For walking away

To Levi,
For understanding

To Ben,
 For everything

Preface

Thank you for opening this book.

No, seriously.
Thank you.

We're delighted that you're here. While we did write this book for almost everyone, we're still glad that you cared enough to pick this book up, peek past the cover, and read what we have to say. We (Kya, her eldest son, Ben, and everyone who helped us develop this book) genuinely appreciate your time and interest.

Because we really do appreciate your time, we tried to keep this book as short as possible. Some may find it difficult to follow and for that we sincerely apologize. Just know that we did try to stick closely to our (admittedly broad) topics; God, life being hard, and how to make life easier, and present the information as efficiently as possible without a lot of chatter and ego.

If you want more chatter and ego, or conversations, updates, and downloads feel free to visit MagickLessons.com.

Despite our best efforts to create a resource that helps all seekers from wherever they are, this book can't be what everyone currently needs. We're perfectly OK with this.

If you feel you may be at risk of harm, from yourself or others, please seek compassionate, local, real world help from somone you can trust.

For those who are skeptical or curious about the origins of this little volume, Kya offers a brief tale of genesis at the end but for now, let's get right to God.

❧ Chapter One ☙
Hey God

God.

Just three little letters. One of the smallest, simplest words, yet humanity insists on using it to describe the infinite mystery of at least one universe. In cultures around the globe, believers in many faiths have stuffed thousands of meanings, stories, and characteristics into this tiny word. It's a bit like an over packed suitcase with so many ideas inside that it's starting to fall apart.

Atheists often look at the confusing contents of this suitcase of a word and throw the entire thing out. Even for believers, using "God" as shorthand for complex, diverse, and vital spiritual concepts keeps us from going deeper into our experiences and learning more from each other when we sit down to discuss the divine.

So first, let's unpack it. After all, it's pointless to shout at God or ask them anything before we can agree on just who and what God is and isn't. Right?

There are plenty of exceptions, but generally speaking there are three broad categories that contain the majority of definitions for what, where and/or who God is:

- ∞ **God the Infinite** - *the Alpha and the Omega*
- ∞ **God the Personal** - *that still, small voice within*
- ∞ **God the King** - *aka God the Father*

We'll discuss each of them, starting with...

✢ God the Infinite ✣

Pantheism - a doctrine that equates God with the forces and laws of the universe

Our first definition of "God" is - **Everything**. The all that is.

One widely agreed upon quality of God is that God is huge. At the very least, God is reported to be bigger and better and smarter than any human. This idea could lead us in a couple of interesting directions, but the one we'll unpack first is rooted in the common belief that God is everywhere. The God that is present in all things is The All That Is.

Pantheism and other spiritual philosophies state that all forms of energy are parts of the divine whole. To a pantheist, nothing is outside of God because God is all that there is or ever can be. In this model, every real and imagined thing in the universe is made of the same sacred material; from tables to wombats, black holes to stars to supernovae. This energy has been called a number of things; life, love, chi, light, prana, flow. It really doesn't matter what we call it.

How do you make an atheist disappear? You define God as the universe. But, once everything is God, what's the point of even having a God? Atheists see nothing as divine, pantheists see everything as divine. In both worldviews, there is no God (or anything else) *outside of* creation. In many ways, these are the exact same beliefs seen through different perspectives.

As we continue to learn more and more about the nature of consciousness, through quantum mechanics and other disciplines, we are discovering that the pantheist perspective seems to offer a better understanding of how our universe actually works. There is more to this talk of vibration and energy and higher consciousness than we've been led to believe and when we understand it, it can change our lives.

When we first discover the perspective that God is everything, it can feel impersonal. It's just energy. It creates everything we are. It is everything that we know. It encompasses every experience we could ever have, and many we couldn't even begin to imagine. Yet, despite actually being us, this version of God has no more concern for humanity than it did for the dodo birds. In a system where everything is a tiny part of a much larger whole, extinction isn't really a concern and the desires of each individual human aren't necessarily going to be honored or even heard.

We can continue to call this energy God but it seems important to recognize that, when we do, we risk confusing those who define God differently from us.

In this book, we're going to refer to this universal energy as magick, mostly because it pleases us to do so. Magick flows, magick is conscious, magick is energy, it has a light side and a shadow side but both are equally divine in nature. Magick is very, very real. We'll talk more about it later on, but for now on to...

ℰ God the Personal ℯ

"The Kingdom of God is within you." - Jesus, Luke 17:21

Our second definition of "God" is - Inner Peace. Nirvana. Bliss. Enlightenment.

Our personal relationships with our gods are both incredibly private and extremely controversial. Those who have a personal relationship with God, however they define it, tend to see God as a close friend, a parent, or even as the highest expression of themselves. This sense of being in close communication with a spiritual consciousness has been an important part of cultures around the globe and is not to be taken lightly.

This personal god isn't a God who is chatting you up from his golden throne in heaven; this is the god/dess that lives within you, the divine in our hearts, beyond logic and fear. This god is our personal brand of ever-evolving magick that comforts and guides us as it encourages us to be more compassionate with ourselves and others.

Some of us are already aware of and communicating with this dimension of divinity and some of us are completely oblivious to it, either way, it's there. We can talk to it, meditate on it, worship and adore it and the more we believe in it, the more we will feel it. It feels like our truest, most loving self.

Unlike our first definition of God - the magick that flows through everything - this definition of God is not completely neutral. It does appear to care about us and our personal desires. Many teachers have told us that we are creators who can create anything we want; we just need to understand how to channel the magick.

To be clear, this personal, divine creator god is a strictly one per customer deal. We run into problems when we start to think that the friendly, wise voice inside our heads is coming to us from outside and needs us to satisfy or serve it. In truth, just like the magick, our personal god does not need for us to be, or do, or have, or experience anything. Nothing at all. All of the needs it has have come directly from us, from our experiences in the world and the way we interact with each other.

The same cannot be said for our next definition of God, and here humanity's hard life problems really begin.

God the King

"The Father has a body of flesh and bones as tangible as man's"

- Doctrine of The Church of Latter-Day Saints (D&C 130:22.)

Our final (for the purposes of this book) definition of "God" is - Invisible Sky King/Father.

This definition is where the rubber really meets the road in terms of atheism versus theism. Are there one or more super beings watching us from above? Do they want us to do something for them? Are ancient books the best source of information we have about them? We'll make our case, then you can decide for yourself. Fair enough?

There is absolutely no way to possibly tell where or when early humans first agreed that there are non-physical, energy beings hanging around wanting to engage with humans, but they did. Early human cultures have virtually universal beliefs in ancestor spirits or angels or messengers or healers or something that could not be seen by those who weren't trained to see them. We could waste time debating which versions of these beings and teachings, if any, were true. Nevertheless, the priests and shamans who were connected to these invisibles held a phenomenal amount of power over the people.

At some point, some of these spiritual leaders began to tell the people tales of invisible kings. There are a thousand reasons to tell a story, who knows why each story developed as it did? Some were very likely meant to serve as cautionary tales, some as examples of virtue, and some, unfortunately, as ways to exploit the gullible and assert power over others.

This particular God definition, one of an invisible creator who rules over and judges humanity, lacks any practical evidence of its existence outside of the human mind. When we examine the idea of an invisible, omnipotent parent/king from a logical, modern perspective there just aren't any good reasons to believe that humanity has ever been in contact with all-powerful beings from *outside* of our universe.

A popular line of thinking states "when you see a watch, you assume a watchmaker designed it, so since the universe is far more complex than a watch, it must have a designer too." This analogy ignores many things, most importantly that watchmakers have parents. Any arguments for deities being external (creatures that exist outside of their creations) invites the idea that such creatures must also have an origin point (a parent or parents), who must also have an origin point, and so on, and so on. Likewise, any argument that the watchmaker "simply is" invites the idea that the watch "simply is", with no watchmaker at all. It's far more likely that our universe is all there is than the alternative, that there are infinite layers of infinite creators creating layers of infinities outside of our infinity.

Another popular argument goes something like this:

Imagine you are alone in a room with two cakes, each one bearing a different sign. The theistic sign reads, "Eat me and a silent, invisible judge will grant you eternal life. If you eat any other cake you will die." The atheistic cake is labeled "You're going to die no matter which cake you eat, but I'm far more delicious than that other cake." This fabled judge may or may not exist but either way; nobody seems willing to offer us any obejective evidence or public advice. How can we choose which cake to eat?

A common response to this dilemma is called Pascal's Wager. Pascal tells us, in essence, "Choose theism. The judge *might* be real, so the shot at potential eternal life is worth a lot more than a few fleeting moments with a tasty cake". On the surface, it's not a bad argument, but Pascal didn't factor in humanity's rich religious diversity. Our long and varied history of religious thought has blessed us with over 4,000 different branches and sects appearing over the past few thousand years, the actual scenario we face today is more like ..:

We are trapped in a vast bakery with not just two, but *thousands* of cakes of varying styles and flavors. As before, each cake bears a sign outlining the various teachings and rules regarding the desires of the invisible judge and most cakes insist that every other cake in the room is poison. The judge(s) in question continue to remain both completely invisible and utterly silent, no matter how long we wait or how loudly we request a hint. How can we possibly choose correctly now?

As most popular theologies state that God loves us unconditionally we are faced with a serious problem. How is it possible that this observing judge loves us, and yet offers us no assistance with the impossible task they have designed for us? Especially if the penalties for our wrong choices are eternal?

Based on our current body of tangible, physical, objective evidence the only answer is, regrettably, that there is no loving invisible father, judge or king out there observing us. No caring parent would devise such a diabolical challenge for their child, nor such dire consequences, especially without giving them clear, consistent, and concise instructions for mastering it.

As long as we cling to our limiting beliefs in the old stories, we will see ourselves as inferior creatures, subject to the whims of (at least one) far superior being. This core belief has been the foundation of countless human systems built to benefit the few at the expense of the many. As we recognize and incorporate the other types of God into our daily lives, we can let go of the false ones and begin to build better systems that uplift all of humanity.

No King, No Slaves, No Masters

When we continue using the word "God" we tap into many irrational thoughts from believers and atheists alike. Anytime the word pops up in conversation, we are given the opportunity to bring clarity by asking people to define it for us. It is interesting to note how many people don't actually know what they mean when they use the word God and have come up with some increasingly fuzzy ideas about what "God" actually is. Asking for a definition offers an exercise in better understanding people and their spiritual beliefs.

As for our own relationship to the spiritual, we can find plenty of evidence for the divine Eternal (rainbows, stardust, and babies) and the divine Internal (joy, peace, and forgiveness), yet no concrete evidence of contact with any divine invisible Kings (no visits from Kali, possessions by Ra, or smitings by Odin).

Therefore,

(unless Bacchus comes down, claims to be The One True Lord, finally gives us the technology for hover cars, and a free puppy, convincing us to revisit this point in light of new evidence...)

if we want our worldview to reflect reality, we must consider that there are no supernatural masters of our fates.

No Zeus, no Odin, no Ra, Jehovah, Oshun, Vishnu, Allah, Shiva… no all-powerful deities. Just very powerful beliefs.

Until we collectively experience something as significant as a visit from on high, we can no longer afford to allow ourselves to be concerned with the pleasing and worshipping of deities who don't care enough about humanity to show up and speak for themselves *(or offer us free puppies)*.

When we let go of our belief in an external, invisible judge of human behavior, we can begin to accept personal responsibility for our choices. Only then can we develop a strong connection to the divine within ourselves as well as the divine that flows through everything.

☙ Chapter Two ❧
Why Is Life So Hard?

Of course, religious thought isn't the only reason for life's hardships. There are plenty of reasons; personal and global, simple and complex, overt and subtle, practical and spiritual. We cannot possibly address all of them here, but we can explore a few of the more disempowering ones.

⚘ Unresolved Childhood Emotions ⚘

Life is hard on everyone, but it's especially hard on children. We are all born ready to learn, looking to our parents to guide us with love and acceptance. We are also born completely helpless, so when our first experiences are hard on us our ability to learn and grow changes, often in unhealthy ways.

Life is especially hard on parents as well. The challenges of raising children in the modern world can lead adults to take out their frustrations in unproductive ways. Like their parents did, because *their* parents did. It's the rare and lucky parent who has the time, energy and ability to listen deeply to their children's every need, respect and address their emotions with compassion, and offer mutually satisfying compromises to every problem.

Instead, parents are strongly encouraged to coerce and mold their precious children into behaving like the compliant adults that society wants them to be.

Newborn mammals of all types communicate their needs with no concern for the needs of others. When subtle signals aren't enough to bring assistance babies cry, loudly, because they know that they deserve to be heard. They know that their needs are important and that, in order for needs to be met, help must be summoned. They don't feel ashamed or afraid to let everyone know that they are unhappy. This is normal, healthy behavior.

Emotionally mature parents will respond to their infant's cries with understanding, kindness, and care. They know that they are their child's first teacher of love and ethical guidance. As children grow and experience the frustrations of walking, locked doors, tying shoes, or not being able to reach treats, they also experience understandable emotional meltdowns. The children of emotionally healthy parents will learn that help is always available. These lucky children are taught new skills for self-expression and self-soothing. As they mature they will stop crying over the minor issues, yet they'll still be able to cry when they're emotionally overwhelmed. As healthy people do.

In unhealthy families, these early experiences are often riddled with shame, fear, and loneliness. Perfectly normal newborn cries are met with anger instead of compassion. As children grow in these families, they may be told that crying is "bad", "selfish" or "manipulative". They often feel that they are spoiled or wrong for seeking attention. They decide that they are defective and unlovable, or worse. The normal upsets of childhood, instead of being processed and overcome, are not adequately addressed (or not addressed at all) causing trauma instead of growth. Children are wired to trust adults, so abused and neglected children often grow up believing that "love hurts". Children raised in violent, blaming and neglectful families tend to become adults with issues ranging from depression to anxiety, substance abuse to self-harm. How many of us feel more connected to fictional characters than to our parents or family because the writers of a book or television show gave us more emotional honesty in their script than anyone in real life ever did?

Even those children fortunate enough to have been raised in warm, nurturing families where their every emotion was cherished may still live in a culture that doesn't value them. Few cultures offer effective structures for processing daily emotional upsets or major traumas. Schools don't tend to care how students feel about homework and employers aren't generally interested in our emotional upsets regarding their policy changes. Instead, there is an expectation of our perpetual happiness in public places with little tolerance for our "bad" emotions. To make things worse, our mental health professionals are often just as emotionally detached and lost as the rest of us.

Global Economic Deception

We generally think that our non-emotional problems are caused by a lack of resources; "There isn't enough money", "I can't find a job", "Everything I earn gets swallowed up in taxes", etc.

Our real problem with money is a highly coercive global economic system.

It's a game designed to keep most of us miserable so that a few can benefit. Like being dealt into a game with complicated and unfair rules, we've been tricked into thinking that the world is supposed to be bought and sold. There must be jobs, profits, losses, economic stability, a gross domestic product, etc. Complex economic rules must be followed any time we make a trade with someone else so that bloated multinational corporations can greedily drain the planet of resources. In the last hundred years we've decided to value the pursuit of profits over life itself, now the bill is coming due.

In the meantime, we are actively encouraged to make critical life decisions based on finances instead of passion, creativity, or joy. We trade what makes us unique for what makes us money as we slowly become more and more disconnected from our dreams, our magick and frequently even our friends and family, as we are forced to commercialize our lives.

It's not a sign of superior moral character to be wealthy. Conversely, it's not our fault if we don't have money, we aren't being punished, we aren't stupid or lazy, the game is rigged and the deck is stacked against us.

Authoritarian Governance

Nowhere is the weight of coercion more tangible than in large scale governing. Authoritarian regimes exist all over the world, we can identify them because they tolerate (or encourage) the suffering of large groups of people whose basic needs for safety, respect, and opportunities to succeed are not being met.

Believers in authoritarian forms of government tell us that the desired result is conformity, that a government that coerces its citizens enough can create order from chaos. We have now had several centuries to allow these authoritarian thinkers to prove that large scale programs of coercion actually do what they have always promised to do. Instead it continues to fail us, to poison us, to degrade us, to take our children in the night. When countries argue that they need to weaponize their police forces against their own citizens, it's time to wake up to the idea that this experiment isn't working as promised.

Authoritarian relationships and families where one family member dominates the others suffer from the same effects of coercion on an intimate scale. Familes with more fluid power structures tend to be happier in general.

Even businesses are recognizing just how damaging and coercive the typical authoritative business environment is. Human-centered corporations have proven to be successful financially as well as socially by focusing on meeting people's needs; not merely those of the customers and the employees, but on those of the community as well.

Our quiet acceptance of and indifference to authoritarianism on every level of society hasn't brought us peace on earth or goodwill. It has brought us drone bombings and child rape and homelessness. The authoritarian experiment has failed us, and it's time to move past it.

Energetic Depression

A growing number of otherwise healthy people are struggling with chronic fatigue or a noticeable lack of energy. Many of us feel like we need caffeine to get us started in the morning or get us through the day. Even if we do have enough energy to complete an eight hour workday, we don't always have anything left at the end of the day to offer our families, our friends, or even ourselves.

In the meantime, western medicine teaches us that our bodies are complex machines that operate by purely mechanical means. Our lack of energy is blamed on chemical imbalances, hormones, mysterious viruses, or the ever popular "stress". Doctors offer us medications and therapy to help us cope with the symptoms, but insist that there is no real "cure" for this puzzling lack of energy in our bodies. So called "alternative" treatments that address the flow of energy through the body are dismissed with words like quackery, delusional or placebo, as if a treatment is only viable if it works in exactly the same way on every single patient.

In fact, we know that our energy levels are closely related to our moods and that people with depression often feel low energy while those who tend to be cheerful frequently feel that they have plenty of energy. The question is, do our moods affect our energy or does our energy level affect our mood? It's a chicken or the egg question with plenty of arguments on either side of the debate, yet the unspoken fact remains that our profit-driven culture of consumption was actively designed to keep us passive and reasonably productive instead of vibrantly alive and filled with joy.

We've been sold false stories about what the human body can and cannot do. We've been conditioned to prefer distractions and appeals to our baser instincts in place of genuine connection and healthy forms of power. We're not being taught how to connect to the magick that flows all around us and we've all but forgotten that this energetic flow is an essential part of maintaining the vibrant health of our minds and bodies.

Health care professionals offer drugs, therapy and exercise plans, but they rarely suggest that we turn off the news, quit our soul-sucking jobs or meditate instead. When their pills don't work we turn to distractions, to drugs, to consumerism, to drama, to therapy or other addictions and wonder why we feel a mysterious "lack of energy" from the minute we wake up until we finally fall asleep.

Until our doctors direct us to connect deeply with our own bodies to ask ourselves what's wrong, until they ask us about our trauma, our coping mechanisms, or our emotional support structures, they don't really see us at all - they're merely looking at our collection of symptoms.

There's a huge difference between treating a cluster of related symptom and witnessing the healing of a human being.

☞ Limiting Ideas About Divinity ☜

Pascal (the guy with the cakes) based his aforementioned wager on the idea that "If you gain, you gain all; if you lose, you lose nothing." While this may have been true back in 1650, we now live in a very different world where the damaging effects of global and domestic religious conflicts have become impossible to ignore. Perhaps, at one time, the development of religious thought was progressive and helped us to create a superior human society. However now, when we mentally separate ourselves from the divine by imagining a solitary "God" living in heaven, we can convince ourselves that inferior humans are nothing more than very clever, but extremely naughty little monkeys who need lots of laws in order to control themselves.

Now that untold generations have adopted and passed down these beliefs, some humans have become so detached from the magick that they can easily poison and hollow out the Earth, if it means they will profit from it. We've even come up with new religious stories about a "new earth" for those who follow the old teachings, further encouraging believers to devalue and devastate our shared planet. They reassure themselves and each other with the idea that they, at least, won't have to suffer the consequences of their actions (or inactions, as the case may be).

Our governments, our economies, our laws, our relationships to nature, our families, our emotional and physical health - all of these systems of belief have grown out of the idea that there is an invisible king in the sky in whose eyes we are merely adorable little sinners.

In fact, nothing could be further from the truth.

We Forgot We Are Magical

When humanity created external deities, we ended up giving them all of our magick powers. The old legends about amazing, magical people who could do incredible things didn't vanish entirely, but we began telling each other that our magick history, despite being repeated to children in every culture all over the planet, is merely a collection of silly faerie tales and nonsense.

But they aren't nonsense after all, they're just slightly exaggerated.

In a world without magick, we see ourselves either as servants of fickle gods or as victims of our circumstances. Because we don't recognize our true power, we blame our environment, the economy, our bodies, and especially each other for everything we fear is wrong with us and the world. Without magick we struggle, we pray, we try to keep our faith, but we never really stand up and take charge of our own lives. We feel too small, too powerless, too trapped.

Once we realize our true magical nature and reclaim our divinity, we can transform our minds, our bodies, our relationships, our families, our communities and our planet.

Until we do, life is stupid hard.

Humanity is on a challenging path. We look to the past; the limitations we learned as children, the values of our ancestors, and the way we feel under constant stress to determine what choices we should make for the future. We know that our parents made mistakes but we choose to minimize them instead of examining and resolving them.

When we're disconnected from our divine nature and taught to see ourselves as powerless, it weakens us both personally and collectively. We continue to develop technologies to connect us with more people but those connections are more likely to be shallow or destructive because we cannot trust ourselves or each other, even those we are closest to. We coerce each other with abandon, even within intimate, so-called "loving" relationships.

Worst of all, we coerce ourselves, because too often it's all we know.

Our Proposal for Humanity

Politics, religion, economic theories, property rights, and self governance are enormous issues and we are not really qualified to offer any expertise on any of them. Instead, we'll just offer an idea.

This idea is poetically expressed in two simple "commandments" that directly mirror each other. Our culture is already starting to accept and work with the first half of the proposal, but the second half is still deeply interwoven into our systems.

We propose that there are only two commandments necessary for a healthier humanity:

Thou shalt actively seek consent
&
Thou shalt not coerce

Coerce: "To compel by force, intimidation, or authority, especially without regard for an individual's desire or volition"

One proposal, two approaches - positive and negative. Ask for permission and stop giving orders. Look for common ground and avoid emotional blackmail. Stand beside other people, not above them.

Communicate more, negotiate more, debate more, force less.

Simple. Not always easy.

Most importantly, we need to begin practicing using more consent and less coercion with the one person in the world we are the hardest on - ourselves. Once we begin to see where we don't always treat ourselves with as much love and respect as we deserve, we can begin to heal our bodies, minds, hearts, and traumas, if we decide to do so.

Chapter Three
An Atheist asks

We've established that our lives are hard because of an abundance of coercion and a lack of consent. Now we can begin to explore some ways to make things easier.

This is probably as good a point as any to remind ourselves that…

Books Don't Have Answers

This book doesn't contain the answers to all of our interpersonal and spiritual problems. How many times have we been told that someone has the perfect solution, be it yoga, meditation, diets, prayer, vision quests, or psychedelic drugs? How many times have we heard some impossibly cheery (and usually financially motivated) person tell us, "If I can do it, anyone can!"? Nonsense. We've all tried something that worked miracles for someone else but didn't do a thing for us.

The fact is there are no one-size-fits-all answers to our most important questions. What works for each person is a blessing for them, but a book about what transformed one life (or a dozen lives, or a thousand) doesn't necessarily hold answers for us.

What books can do is offer new information to help us unlock the answers buried within ourselves. That's where most of the answers we need are usually found, within us. The rest of the answers we need are in the other people around us, not books.

Books and teachers alike can and do offer us important insights. Some books offer ideas powerful enough to change our minds, giving us new perspectives on life. These changes can bring us closer to understanding ourselves and each other or further away from each other. Engaging our hearts along with our minds while we read allows us to better filter the inspirational treasures from the dehumanizing trash. When we keep choosing the ideas that bring us closer together, we can begin to find new solutions to old problems.

Any overly complicated or uncomfortable solutions to our problems are best ignored though. It doesn't matter how nice my hammer is, it's not likely to fix my leaky toilet. Hammers are great tools, exercise is a great tool, hypnosis is a great tool, but if they don't fit our current needs, they may do us more harm than good.

Soup

At some point in the last several years, the "Law of Attraction" gained popular acceptance. This law states that life doesn't just randomly happen to us, but that the world around us responds to our thoughts and that we see more of whatever we choose to focus on. Like the word God, this idea is often packed in with other, more dubious claims like "we create our own reality" or that humans are designed to simply manifest any material possession they want. These claims often lack a basic understanding of several things, not the least of which would be the gross inequalities designed into our current social systems.

So let's be clear -

We did not "create" the reality that we were born into. ❧

We were all born into cultures, families, and systems that existed long before we fell into them. We were added to an already dynamic vibration, like a single, new ingredient freshly dropped into a rich and complex soup.

Everybody's soup is a little different. Some people's soups are almost nothing like each other's; a child born into wealth, education and respect is part of a much different soup than the child born into poverty, addiction and violence.

There's nothing we can do now to change the soup we were born into, that ship has sailed. However, we can work to improve the flavor of the soup that we're currently in. That's what reasonable people mean when they talk about "creating our own reality".

We can absolutely add and subtract ingredients from today's soup. We can develop new interests and relationships, stop talking to people who don't value us, start walking in the woods, change our wardrobe, attend an interesting sounding meeting or class. Depending on our creativity and support, there are countless ways to move forward from where we are right now, whether we were born into a rich lobster bisque or a complex minestrone, a spicy chili or a simple broth.

❧ *As we integrate, we accept more and more responsibility for the soups we chose but that's a conversation for another day.*

Communication

Relationships are the most important parts of our lives. Communication is the most important part our all of our relationships. It is absolutely vital that we all learn how to communicate respectfully and honestly with ourselves and with each other.

Our personal soup defines our unique perspective on the world. Not all people see "reality" as we do. Those of us raised in cultures that valued freedom learned to see and speak about commitments differently from those raised in cultures that valued obedience. Families that enjoy a variety of outdoor sports think differently about their physical bodies than those who are competitively focused on a single activity, especially if that activity is reading, or playing the piano instead of playing tennis.

The first step to improving our communication with others is to assume as little as possible about the people we're talking to. We may or may not share a common perspective and be speaking the same language. It's really only safe to assume that everyone is swimming around in their own flavor of soup, not always aware of just how isolating that can be.

We want to connect to each other, to bond, to enhance each other's lives, and bring out the best in our relationships. The fastest way to do that is to realize that everyone everywhere has two universal things in common - needs and feelings. Healthy, respectful, balanced communication begins when we recognize that we're all just trying to get our needs met and our feelings acknowledged.

Whenever we are in conflict with someone, it's a good bet that someone's needs are not being met, or their feelings are not being honored.

As with our earlier sense of consent and coercion being two parts of the same whole, communication also consists of two inseparable forces, an inhale and an exhale if you will. We **speak** and we **listen**. Most of us need to work on both skills, especially those of us who grew up in soups where even the smallest of conflicts resulted in the use of angry words. We are now choosing to speak without judgment or blame, and listen in ways that honor and meet the needs of others, not merely our own.

Speaking

When we speak, we tend to share a few basic things, mostly; **facts**, **opinions**, **observations**, and **judgments**. Human beings are naturally curious and observant creatures. Our brains are designed to gather data and form opinions. When those opinions are shared by enough people and backed with enough evidence, we can consider them to be facts, but changes in perspective often reveal that one culture's "facts" are nothing more than their popular opinions. Judgments, however, are little more than elevated opinions that act as a poison in healthy relationships.

To review, **facts** are facts; they're objective and not emotional. For example, "Your unwashed clothing is on the floor". This is a statement of fact. It's not an opinion or a judgment. It either is or isn't true and anyone who looks at the floor should be able to confirm (or deny) it. When we communicate in nothing but facts, our conversations are productive and respectful, if a little dry.

Opinions and **observations**, unlike facts, vary from person to person, as in, "This room looks messy". Not everyone will agree that the room looks messy, it's not a fact. One soup's mess is another soup's system, but that's the beauty of it all. We don't have to all agree, in fact, we can't all agree, it's neither likely nor desirable for humanity to strive for uniformity. We're going to continue to be a collection of different people, swimming around in different soups, wanting different things from life and adding different opinions to the conversation. Sharing our opinions respectfully allows us all to engage more fully and bring our desires to the table, building deeper, healthier relationships, and developing new, better systems to support us all as we look toward our collective future.

Judgments, on the other hand, are never helpful. Judgments are opinions that contain a painful hook in the form of an implied absolute right and wrong. For example, "Nobody should live like this." The topic has been opened and closed with no room for debate. We dehumanize each other, even children, by passing judgments and most of us are barely even aware that we do it. How many times do children hear things like, "You live like a pig"? What does hearing such harsh things teach children about how they should feel about themselves?

Despite our best intentions, judging others always causes harm, both to the other person and to our relationship with them. Whenever we feel judged we want to defend ourselves, so one judgment frequently leads to another, "You're being ridiculous"… and another argument begins.

When we are careful to stick to communicating with facts and respectful opinions, we can be honest without being unkind. **Researching our facts**, taking whole hearted **ownership of our own opinions and observations,** and **examining our judgments** without expressing them is a three-fold path to speaking with integrity.

Listening

If speaking is the exhale of communication, listening is the inhale. Without inhaling, breathing doesn't work as designed. Without listening, communication doesn't work either.

Listening doesn't mean just kicking back and letting folks vent at us while we nod and smile, it means putting aside our needs and feelings as we explore the needs and feels of others. The three-fold path for listening consists of; **holding space**, **reflecting** and **encouraging**.

Holding space is the silent part of the practice that we universally recognize as listening. It requires our focused attention, a vital skill that is being modeled less and less in our modern culture. Attention is best focused in three different areas; our eyes, our heart, and our soul connections. When we consciously choose to connect in all three centers while engaging, we can fully support others as they choose to open up to us. Our mental communication checklist should occasionally remind us to maintain eye contact, open our hearts to their hearts and recognize the magick that flows through us both as we listen to them speak.

Reflecting creates healthy, positive relationships, *projecting* does not. Knowing the difference is critical. Reflecting is the time when we repeat back what we have heard in order to make certain that we truly understand what's being said. This practice can involve simply repeating word for word what was just said, or paraphrasing what we think we heard and what we think it might mean. Reflecting is an art form all its own. It's a crucial skill for building solid relationships as it helps us bridge the inevitable gaps between what was said, what was meant, and what was heard. Those pesky gaps have been known to swallow relationships whole if we don't work to close them through endless rounds of reflecting.

Once we've offered a reflection to our conversation partner, we follow it up by holding space for them again. This allows them to either agree with our reflection or correct us when we've misunderstood them. If we are corrected we simply THANK the speaker, reflect the correction and move to another phase of listening (not speaking), in order to honor their contribution to our continued growth.

Encouraging is the master listener's secret weapon. Secret because it's so frequently underused and weapon because it is extremely powerful. Another of our two part tools, we encourage others both through **praise** and by **asking questions**.

Praise is expressed through our words of encouragement, compliments, love, and appreciation for another person. Everyone enjoys being praised, even if they don't know exactly how to process it when the praise is being offered.

Questions are the holy grail of listening skills. Knowing how to ask good questions can transform a fairly good conversation into the beginning of a long, deep relationship. People love to be asked about the things that they love. If everything else fails, we can always ask, "What do you really enjoy doing?" and see what happens to our relationship next.

Our Inner Dialogue

From the conversations in our lives to the conversations in our heads, we also need to work on addressing and improving our own self-talk; our inner thoughts and comments about ourselves and our behaviors. When others don't listen to us or ignore our needs we tend to notice it, but when we're the ones ignoring our own needs, it can be trickier to see it.

Depending on the soup we were born into, we usually develop some kind of inner dialogue as we grow. This dialogue often features voices that say things very similar to the things our adult role models and peers said when we were young. Some voices are kind, some doubt our abilities, and others can be just plain cruel. Phrases from the past can replay in our minds decades later, pretending to be our own brand new thoughts about a current issue in our lives.

If we don't have an inner dialogue, or if it's always supportive and loving, we won't need to worry about it much, but many of us have absorbed the negative judgments of our critics so completely that their words still echo in our brains today. Modern psychology acknowledges the idea of an "inner critic" who can be motivating or destructive, depending on how they've been constructed and what they've been constructed from. Only we can know if we are hosting unwanted ghosts from our pasts in our minds, but if we don't truly, madly and deeply love our deliciously divine selves yet, we probably are.

Some of us will find it hard to even understand self-compassion, much less practice it regularly. For us it can be easier to begin by imagining we're talking to a beloved child, lover or family member when we "talk" to ourselves.

**"Good morning, my darling!
Welcome to a beautiful new day!"**

**"Let's make sure you get
some water and a healthy breakfast
before you leave the house."**

**"You're doing great.
Time for a victory dance!"**

**"Oops, that didn't work.
OK, don't worry, we'll fix it."**

**"It's all right now."
"Everything's fine."**

"You've got this!"

"YES!"

How different would our day be if we had a fun, supportive, loving inner voice constantly cheering by our side?

"We have never felt better!"

"Everything is working out perfectly"

As we develop healthier self-talk and discover what authentically taking care of ourselves feels like, our ability to create healthier relationships with others will bloom as well.

The Placebo Effect

A placebo is a substance that scientists consider unable to cause any measurable effect on an experiment. In health-related experiments placebos are used to "blind" both researchers and patients so neither knows if the pill they are taking is a pharmaceutical or not. Presumably placebos don't have the power to make people's symptoms better, but they do. All the time. Scientists call it the placebo effect and, honestly, they find it kind of annoying. It has a tendency to ruin perfectly good experiments when too many patients respond to the placebo.

The lesson here is that when humans believe something can heal them, they often have the power to make it heal them, even when there's no objective reason why it should. So it's no surprise that the people who believe in yoga tend to find yoga healing for them. It also follows that people with no interest in yoga are probably going to be less likely to benefit from it.

There's no logical reason to believe that crystals protect us from "negative energies", but there's no question that some people really do feel more positive when they carry crystals around in pouches and pockets. We could argue with these people, giving them our "facts" and explaining to them that there's no reason to believe their crystals actually do anything, but why? We humans were blessed with the extraordinary ability to think, to believe, to faith our way into any number of ideas both brilliant and questionable. Why not use our big, powerful brains to believe our way into health, and happiness, and abundance?

It sounds easy, but of course it isn't. We all know that.

Simple maybe, but not easy.

Swapping out our old, self-deprecating beliefs for shiny happy new ones is hard. It's simple to repeat an affirmation. "I am strong, I am strong, I am strong", I may gasp as I wheeze my way up the stairs. Do I believe it? How do I know? How do I feel? If I am filled with joy and feel healthy and strong as I huff and puff my way forward, I can feel it, I know it, and I believe it. But if I'm merely repeating an empty affirmation or mantra, I could tell myself I'm powerful and strong and healthy all day long while my mind conjured up images of ambulance rides and life insurance policies, forgotten gym memberships and broken promises. It doesn't matter what we are saying if we don't believe in it. We become what we believe we are, not what we say we believe we are.

There's a huge difference.

In this way, our healing process is a bit like building a house. If we want to have a solid foundation, we need to start right where we are. We cannot build anything substantial until we've cleared away the old debris. Letting go of our outdated or unfocused beliefs allows us to make room for new, solid, positive focused ideas. With the right tools, we can make progress, but only if we actually do the work.

When consciously invoked, the placebo effect can be a highly effective tool for healing. We just need to take the time to identify what we actually believe in. It takes focus and effort but with some practice, it has the potential to transform every facet of our lives… if we believe it can.

Chapter Four
God answers

God is universal and God is personal. God is internal and God is external, but never truly separate from me. God speaks to me every day because I consciously take the time to sit and listen in meditation every day. We all share a universal God, but none of us shares a personal God. Mine is mine, yours is yours. I discover mine through my meditations; you are free to discover yours through any path you feel drawn to.

There's no big reveal here where I tell you what God told me to tell you to do. It doesn't work like that. God answered me. God will answer you. You simply need to ask.

More and more people are being drawn to the idea of a spiritual awakening. We believe we are experiencing profound spiritual insights. We're not alone in this belief and many teachers and students offer us "truths". Some of these "truths" appear to contradict each other, causing tension and resulting in judgements. Since we know this kind of thinking isn't helpful, we offer the following metaphors to help remind ourselves exactly what is happening and where we are going as we travel our new, enlightened spiritual paths.

☞ Merely Sprouts ☜

Imagine that each human being is a single seed in a big wooden box. These seeds are hanging out, rattling around together, bumping into each other, making a bunch of noise, but not actually doing anything very important. With no dirt and no water, they're just seeds. They hold the potential for an amazing life inside each one of them but they ain't woke.

Not yet.

Now imagine one seed being isolated from the others and dropped into the dirt. Trapped, lost, confused. That's how so many of us come to our spiritual awakenings; feeling like we've been buried alive, alone in our pain, thrown into the dirt. The infamous "rock bottom" so many recovering addicts speak of.

Then comes water. It might be meditation, or counseling, or spiritual healing. It might come from a book or a website, but it nourishes that tiny spark of magick inside of us. It helps us to break open our shell, if only a little bit.

We can still hear the noises made by the community of seeds we were once part of, but as we learn more about ourselves and the true nature of life, we find that we listen to them less and less. They will learn or they will not learn, as they choose. They are all infinitely precious and rare and irreplaceable, and yet, they are each merely one of an endless supply of seeds.

As new spiritual sprouts, we join countless thousands of people around the world who consider themselves to be "awakened" or "enlightened" or even a guru, a god or goddess. Our awakening experiences are so powerful and leave us so detached from everything we once understood about life that many new sprouts believe that they must be fully grown plants.

They claim fancy titles and preach of the glories that their water has brought them. We can expect nothing more nor less from a bunch of sprouting seeds who know nothing but whispers about their future of sun, wind, and harvest.

They still ain't woke... yet.

As we continue to grow from noisy little seeds into fully grown plants of our own, there are a great many new experiences along the way. With each success, there is a tendency to think "Wow, I understand so much more now than I did before. Surely this is enlightenment!"

Silly sprout. There will always be more to come, more room to grow, and more to learn. Enlightenment isn't a destination, enlightenment is an ever-expanding perspective that we're either experiencing in any given moment or we're not. The tiny sprout reaches enlightenment and feels the bliss of it, then tumbles into conflict and curses it as it strives to return to the state of bliss. The mighty tree feels the bliss of enlightenment and the bliss of tumbling into and out of conflict, again and again and again.

Be wary of those who claim to have all the answers.

Most of them don't even have all of the questions ... yet.

Our Inner Prism

Every spiritual seeker that has ever walked the planet has developed their own sense of their divine inner core. This primal fire has been called by countless names; soul, essence, anima, life force, inner being.

For those of us who offer spiritual insights through the use of soup metaphors, it serves us to picture our eternal souls as prisms (ideally one of those large faceted crystal balls that conjures an ocean of rainbows from a single sunbeam, those are fun). Once we remember how to open ourselves up to the magick that flows all around us, our own prisms begin to radiate all kinds of wonderful things into our lives.

In fact, that's the way we all come into this world; clear, divine, innocent, perfect, and eager to learn more. Each one of us knowing that we're a rare, unique ingredient in this vast cosmic soup. We are one with the magick, deliberately choosing to animate a new body that will explore a universe full of feelings and a handful of needs. We are love and flow and laughter and delight.

Then,
our happy little butts
splashdown
right in the middle
of
our family's
soup.

While some of us were genuinely welcomed as the visiting angels that we literally are, far too many of us were not. Either way, none of us floated through life on cotton candy clouds of bliss. The process of becoming human hurts. Life is messy and boring and loud and big and, eventually, everyone cries for help and finds themselves alone. Whether we've been pampered our entire lives or we fought over scraps in the streets, every time we encounter an idea that our prism knows to be untrue, it hurts.

We can see this clearly in babies who protest at even the mildest discomfort or frustration. They've stepped out of the bliss and into hunger and confusion and cold and they're stuck until their need is either resolved or rewired. Recognizing our needs, expressing them and resolving them is the natural cycle of life. We feel hungry, we eat, we feel satisfied, the flow of magick through our prism continues and we move on to identifying a new need. But when needs go unmet, when we can't resolve them and maintain our connection to the magick, we have to adapt. Rewiring is our brain's way of redirecting energy when it can't be resolved.

Rewiring doesn't affect the prism, it's still clear and pure and gorgeous. It doesn't affect the magick that continues to flow everywhere as it always has and always will. Rewiring only affects our brain. It redirects our attention away from the need our prism is expressing. Like casting a shadow that protects us from a blinding light, our mind attempts to protect us from the pain of our unmet needs by blocking some of the flow of magick and reducing the intensity of the bond between our minds and our prisms. In this crude way, we comforted ourselves when there was no comfort. In time, we learned to live without the magick, the vitality, the joy we used to be. In time we accepted that our needs didn't matter as much as someone else's needs mattered.

But prisms don't dissolve, not even in the harshest of soups, they remain beautiful and connected to the magick and patiently waiting for us to finally stop rewiring ourselves and begin to resolve our inner conflicts instead. When we know better, we can choose to do better. We do better when we realize that we are not broken, we simply got some wires crossed 20, 40, 70 years ago when we needed something and it never came. We survived, we adapted, we moved on, but we lost faith. We convinced ourselves that we preferred the shadows to the light. Maybe not always, maybe not a lot, but sometimes we forget that we're actually a constant flow of eternal love passing through this temporary body.

Hey, it happens.

Thankfully, the process for resolving emotions and clearing old shadows is fairly simple to teach, even though it rarely feels easy to implement. Practice and patience are always good places to start learning anything new. However in this case, the most important word is perfect, as in; We are all perfect exactly as we are and we've freaking got this!

As long as the the idea of perfection isn't being used as an excuse for standing still and simply accepting the pain we feel as "perfect", as long as we continue to focus on moving toward a clearer, more radiant prism and a closer connection to the magick, we do well to remind ourselves joyfully and often, just how delightfully perfect we really are.

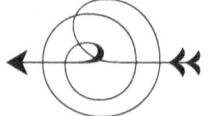

:

ಬ Chapter Five ಜ
Magick Lessons

Magick is the word we chose to represent the divine energy that flows through all things. Like an uplifting radio broadcast in search of a receiver, magick flows around us everywhere we go. We can tune ourselves into any number of different frequencies, but when we consciously align ourselves with magick our potential; for healing, for learning, for living a life that isn't hard, increases dramatically.

As we've mentioned, the process for tuning into the magick is a matter of changing ourselves instead of trying to change other people, or the world around us. This doesn't mean that we blindly accept everything, even abuse, with loving good humor. It does mean that we identify our feelings and needs, take any sensations of discomfort seriously and choose what makes us feel better, instead of worse. Every time we choose ourselves and our sense of faith and connection over the old stories of drama and pain, we learn another powerful lesson in magick.

As we realign ourselves with the flow of magick through our lives and bodies, we inhale, expanding our capacity and increasing our vibrations through Light Work. Our exhale is the Shadow Work that allows us to examine and release all of the rewired circuits we cobbled together decades ago. Despite centuries of misinformation about magicians who embrace the shadows, true students of magick know that both practices are equally important to the enlightenment we all seek.

Light Work

This is fun side of healing, the part that feels good and can be discussed in "polite company". Light work is any exercise or technique that increases our vibration; meditation, sculpting, yoga, playing around, affirmations, dance, laughter, gratitude journals, etc. It's anything that brings more "light" into a situation and makes us feel happier, more vibrant, more alive.

The light is selfish. Don't be surprised, we all want to do many things that we've been told our entire lives we shouldn't do.

We need to do those things.

Seriously, enjoy them. We start with things that don't feel too outrageous, like wearing the clothes we like, going places that feel welcoming, and eating the food that genuinely pleases us. Self-care starts with throwing away the rules that other people made about how we should care for ourselves. We are the ultimate experts on the subject of ourselves - our bodies, our thoughts, our vibration. We need to trust that when we commit to doing things our way, we won't go wrong.

More than that, we need to recognize that when we increase our vibration and allow magick to flow into our lives, we help raise the vibration of our families, our communities and our planet. Maybe not by a lot, but by enough to make a difference in the lives around us. Our joy is contagious and when we focus on increasing our own joy, we can't help but bring others joy as well.

It is worth noting that, while most of the experience of increasing our frequency and vibration is pleasant, some of us do experience mild "power surges" as we open old connections and resolve old issues. These surges can be uncomfortable, especially if we resist them, but with focus and acceptance our bodies will adjust to the new flow.

Simple Light Work Tools

Music

Music grants us the power to depress and anger ourselves or uplift and encourage ourselves or anything in between. Singing, playing an instrument, or even just listening to an inspiring song is basic light work.

Because we all have different vibrations, we react to music, frequencies, and rhythms in different ways. We feel emotional, we move, pulsing, our hips shake, our arms wave, our throats clench, we laugh, we howl, we cry. Two people exposed to the same song can have two completely different reactions as the vibrations of the song activate our personal vibrations, creating a harmonic as unique as we are.

By paying attention to the ways music affects us and the people around us, we can use it to bring more positivity, joy, and ease into our lives.

Sleep

For some sleep comes easy, for others, it's a challenge. We don't usually think of sleeping as light work, but our ancestors knew sleep to be a powerful method of healing, both physically and emotionally.

Many of us were rewired to believe that all people need a specific amount of sleep. Fortunately, life is not a one-size-fits-all activity. When we honor our natural rhythms our bodies tell us when to rest and when to wake. Obviously, those of us in the clutches of an inflexible work schedule will have more difficulty discovering those long forgotten rhythms, but find them we can.

We honor our bodies by focusing on creating a sleeping sanctuary, a place of serenity, safety and rest. When we measure our sleeping area in terms of serenity, we're not just talking about the obvious physical space, the bedding, lighting, and decor, but also at our energy when we enter, leave and relax in that space.

Coming in to our sleeping space, we can remind ourselves of the joys of the day. Forgiving ourselves and everyone else for any conflicts or disappointments, we tune ourselves to the frequency of healing, restful sleep that prepares us for an even better tomorrow.

On rising, we can acknowledge the blessings of the night, both conscious and subconscious, affirm our health, meditate, and prepare ourselves for another successful day ahead.

Food

Most things in creation spend the better part of their days pursuing food. Humans are no different. Food is such a complex part of our lives that it offers us opportunities for both light and shadow work. Any rewiring we did in our past involving; what tastes good, what we deserve to eat, the various sources of our food, making different food choices, diets, holiday foods and anything else has the potential to activate at any point, often requiring shadow work processes to resolve any misdirected emotions. We should be prepared to face needs and feelings we may have spent a lifetime avoiding. If our relationship with food is especially troubled, we may choose to work with others in order to navigate our way through the challenges.

Magick creates food, is food, consumes food, ripens food, spoils food, hunts food, devours food and above all delights in the beauty and power of the entire food chain from the smallest planktons to the deadliest beasts. It's an eternal dance that has always and will always require a great deal of "sacrifice" in terms of living bodies becoming food for other living bodies. If magick could express general concerns about our relationship to food, it wouldn't center on sacrifice (which is natural and inevitable), but on suffering (which is not).

Prisms know exactly what foods our bodies need. Foods are our prism's friends, not our enemies (as we are so often encouraged to see them). Light work theory teaches us to listen to our cravings, get comfortable with eating whatever we enjoy eating, and celebrate the pleasures of eating.

Our larger cultural soup is filled with endless rewirings on the topic of food. Most of us are familiar with the shadowy feeling of eating something "healthy" that we don't actually enjoy or, better yet, the shameful feeling of enjoying something "unhealthy". When we choose to eat whatever we really, truly want with gratitude, joy and the intention that it will nourish us both body and soul, we are performing light work and doing ourselves a world of good.

And so on. There are countless paths for light work and infinite ways to increase our vibration. As we progress, new ideas will naturally occur to us and inspire further explorations.

Shadow Work

The less popular, more uncomfortable and often neglected side of healing, shadow work focuses on the emotions and traits that we'd prefer to keep hidden. Exposing and addressing our shadow side is an essential part of spiritual development that cannot be bypassed.

Our shadow issues are largely the result of rewiring experiences in the brain, battle scars from a childhood (and beyond) where we struggled to learn how to fit in and when to stand out. These are the places where we had needs that couldn't be met and we had to turn away from the magick for our own protection. Now that we are safe, it's time to rewire ourselves and let our magick flow again.

Shadow work is messy. It's intense. It tends to be isolating because other people don't want to deal with our grief and fear (honestly, they really don't want to deal with their own). It's highly spiritual, extremely important and frequently shunned, degraded or shamed as not being "good", positive or uplifting.

Working with shadows is incredibly positive and uplifting… once the rewiring is resolved and the process is complete. It's only when we get stuck in our shadows and reactivate the same traumas over and over without making progress that we make shadow work look and feel like hell. Those who understand how to step all the way through the process to a satisfying resolution find shadow work to be an effective way of letting go of outdated beliefs and stepping back into alignment with the divine.

Recognizing our rewired feelings and thoughts requires us to be completely honest with ourselves about what we want. Our feelings and emotions guide us towards a better life when we are honestly processing and expressing all of them, from shame to compassion, sorrow to joy, from fear to love.

There are many different processes out there for shadow work, it would be impossible to cover them all in this book. One process is described at the end of the next chapter for those who feel drawn to it.

Embracing and healing ourselves is the first step on the path to healing our wounded world. Through our own healing, we inspire others to heal. Leave behind the old archetype of the wounded healer, as those who don't know who and what they truly are will be unable to awaken that knowledge in others.

∞ Chapter Six ∞
Exercises

The following exercises, including the shadow work process at the end, are suggestions for steps in the lifelong process of rewiring our minds and resolving our emotions. Feel free to decide for yourself which parts of each exercise sound helpful for your journey and which should be adapted or discarded.

Exercises with a meditation are highlighted to be read more easily. Consider recording them and playing them back at your leisure.

- **Before beginning any exercise, set a personal intention in alignment with your needs (e.g. "I do this for myself and for the highest good of all concerned").**

- **Check-in frequently with your intuition for guidance on how to proceed.**

- **Assume that you know exactly what you need and act accordingly.**

Exercises

- There is no right or wrong way to process our emotions, only ways that get us closer to the outcome we ultimately want and ways that don't.

- When in doubt, focus on your intentions, not the form of the exercise.

Exercise One
Inhale Magick, Exhale Magic
Suggested - Daily

This is an extremely simple but powerful practice; if you can breathe you can do this. Twenty minutes a day is suggested and brings results for most people. More or less time invested may vary the results experienced.

If the word magick doesn't appeal, substitute another like "energy" or "love". Whether magick or placebo, this exercise reminds us that energy flows in, around, and through us at all times.

Relax your body completely, either sitting or lying down.

Close your eyes and inhale.

Feel the magick entering your nostrils, throat, chest, lungs, belly, filling you with magick.

Ignoring and releasing all other thoughts, focus only on the abundant, flowing magical energy coming into your body.

On the exhale, relax and send your own unique magical frequency out of your body through your breath, back into the world.

Exercise One

Inhale and exhale, nothing else. Focus on the energy in every breath you take.

This exercise in not thinking is challenging at first but with regular practice, your focus will improve and the results can give you a delightful escape from the mundane.

Though presented here as a classic, silent meditation, this practice is also powerful when combined with any kind of enjoyable physical activity. In fact, it has a tendency to make even the most mundane physical activities far more enjoyable!

You can use two different ideas, one for the inhale and a different one for the exhale, however to experience this light work technique as intended, avoid using "negative" terms on the exhale (fear, shame, pain, etc.). The less focus we put into the idea of having pain or doubt to be released, the less we attract it. There is a time and place to practice balance between our light and shadow sides but this exercise isn't it.

Exercise Two
Magick Above, Magick Below
Suggested - Daily

If the idea of magick still sounds odd, consider that the Sun and the core of the Earth are two obvious, powerful natural sources of energy in our lives. Connecting ourselves to both of these energy sources gives many of us a sense of power. The energy of the Earth is a grounding, primal power. The energy of the Sun (or whatever non-physical source of spiritual energy you prefer to identify with) is expansive, visionary and divine in nature. When we connect to one and not the other, we can become unbalanced.

This exercise helps bring in both energies to charge us up and put us back into balance and harmony with the flow of magick through our bodies and lives.

Breathe. In and out. In and out.

Focus your attention on the lower parts of your body: your feet, legs, the very base of your spine. Feel the energy in your body. Feel that energy moving through your physical body.

Let yourself expand and harmonize with your magick body. You are so much bigger than your physical body, your magick body grows

and moves out and down. Down through the floor, into the earth and down, down, down, right to the very center of the earth and the massive ball of molten energy at its core. Feel your energy connect to the energy of the earth.

Feel it glow and grow as it rockets back to fill your toes, knees, and hips. Feel the grounding energy of the planet move up into your belly, your spine, up into your chest, your heart. Feel your heart filling with the passion and fire of the earth.

Follow the energy up and down each arm, through your neck, into your head and feel it arrive at the crown of your head. Your body is grounded, and relaxed.

Let the energy of the Earth keep moving up, past the crown of your head and up, through the ceiling, into the sky, beyond earth's atmosphere. Keep moving your awareness up until you connect with the energy that calls to you.

This power is ready to connect to you, ready to send a flood of raw power back down into the crown of your head. Feel it purify and heal you as it flows into your head, your eyes, your jaw.

Warming, relaxing, releasing, cleansing as it moves further down into your throat, your shoulders, down your arms and into each powerful finger.

Feel it strengthen and charge your spine, feel the energy of above meet and mingle with the energy from below as it flows into your chest.

Focus on the glowing, perfect synthesis of energies that are now pulsing and expanding in your heart.

As written, this is a complete exercise for grounding and connecting. It can also be the first stage of a deeper meditation, including exercises 8 and 9 in this book.

Not everyone is able to feel their connection to these energies right away. If the energy isn't flowing for you or you feel blocked, try moving your body, either a little or a lot instead of trying to stay still. The next exercise tends to help us feel the energy as well.

Exercise Three
Divine Dance Party
Suggested - Daily

Inspiring music and intuitive movement are both excellent ways to increase our vibrations. By combining them both, we can create a flexible, personalized ritual for both solo and group activities.

Choose music that inspires you to move your body, whatever that music may be. If your favorite songs make your body move and smile and play and dance, use them. The "ideal" songs for this practice have strong beats without lyrics to distract us from the conversation we're having with our bodies. If you don't have a lot of instrumental jams in your collection and want to explore some options, try searching your favorite source for "traditional music" or "world music". Choose pieces from the musical styles that call out to your body and make you want to wiggle!

Start where you are with what you have. If you need to dance in a chair or holding on to the wall, do that. Intuitive movement is excellent for those of us with physical challenges because it meets us exactly where we are today. Can't get out of bed? Just listen to the music and move whatever moves. When we are addressing physical challenges, we can get so focused on trying to make our bodies do what our minds want them to do that we forget to relax and spend time allowing our bodies to do what they want to do instead.

Combine several pieces of upbeat, instrumental music into a playlist that lasts from anywhere from 15 minutes to an hour and dance to it regularly.

Set your intention on your very highest good and just move. No rules, no steps, no predetermined rhythm or tempo, just move your body to the music in whatever way your body wants to flow.

If the flow of energy through your body feels blocked anywhere, pay attention and work with the music and the energy and your body to restore as much flow as possible. Know that, with enough time and faith in the process, energetic flow can be recovered.

For bonus points, try to keep your mind from thinking about anything except the dance you are dancing. At the very least, try not to get so caught up in your thinking that you ignore your body's messages like pain and tension. Go easy on your body when it needs rest and praise yourself for taking such good care of yourself, even when that means modifying movements, slowing down or taking a break.

Hydrate. It's important.

Exercise Three

Sometimes we realize that our old favorite songs aren't really all that positive or inspiring. A lot of popular music glorifies pain and keeps us stuck in thoughts about our past mistakes. If you find this is the case with your musical preferences (and you don't want to be stuck listening to nothing but Peruvian drums and sitar music all day) there are a number of high energy pop songs to inspire us.

Consider making at least one "inspirational" playlist of songs that remind you of who you truly are and why you are here. At the risk of exposing our limited knowledge of music, Iwe offer the following suggestions that tend to uplift us when we're down.

<u>Happy Pop:</u>

- Queen - Don't Stop Me Now
- Abba - Dancing Queen
- The Kinks - Get Up & Better Things
- The Who - Fragments
- The Rolling Stones - Shine A Light
- Bob Marley - Three Little Birds
- Nahko - Mitakuye Oyasin
- Louis Armstrong - What A Wonderful World
- Martha & The Vandellas - Dancing in the Streets
- Tegan and Sara - Everything Is Awesome
- The Beach Boys - Good Vibrations
- Cyndi Lauper - Girls Just Wanna Have Fun
- Katrina & The Waves - Walking on Sunshine
- Justin Timberlake - Can't Stop The Feeling!
- Rachel Platten - Fight Song
- Pharrell Williams - Happy

Hey God, Why Is Life So Hard?

- Sara Bareilles - Brave
- Katy Perry - Roar
- Taylor Swift - Shake It Off
- The Black Eyed Peas - I Gotta Feeling
- Jimmy Cliff - You Can Get It If You Really Want
- I Fight Dragons - Time To Fly
- Janelle Monae - Tightrope
- Michael Franti & Spearhead - I'm Alive
- Matisyahu - One Day
- Saara Alto - Monsters

Exercise Four

Appreciation
Suggested - Daily

As we wake up each day and as we close our eyes each night, let us give thanks and appreciate our many blessings. Rituals are helpful reminders to take some time out and focus on all the good in our lives. Examples of appreciation rituals include:

- Offering a simple thought of appreciation for all of the energy that went into growing and preparing the meal we're about to eat.

- Reciting a list of all the things we're thankful for.

- Writing an entry of three new things we're grateful for in an Appreciation Journal.

- Complimenting and/or appreciating five people a day.

- Complimenting ourselves five times before breakfast.

- Celebrating the simple pleasures in life

The most effective rituals are the ones that genuinely inspire us and the ones we will actually perform. There's little point in developing a ritual around something that we don't honestly appreciate, nor in creating an overly elaborate ritual that stresses us out. If we start with something that means a great deal to us, it's often easier to remember, and want to, and actually do it.

Adopt an appreciation ritual to perform every day as you're waking up.

Adopt an appreciation ritual to perform every day as you're going to sleep.

Adopt more rituals of appreciation to perform between the first two rituals as desired.

Results will vary based on intentions and intensity, but do be careful. It's easy to fall prey to the classic trap of kicking ourselves because we're not grateful enough. The most important person to appreciate is you.

There is a sample page for an appreciation journal on page 96 and available for download on MagickLessons.com.

Exercise Five
How Great Would That Be?
Suggested - Daily

This is a flexible thought exercise to practice either alone or with others. Imagination is the key to enhancing our positive thoughts and feelings and charging up our energy.

Catch yourself thinking a negative thought. Something like "That's stupid" or "I hate my job".

Play "How great would it be…?" and turn the negativity around.

How great would it be if everything worked perfectly?

How great would it be to have a job that I love?

How great would it be to feel like my work is making a real difference in people's lives?

How great would it be if I didn't have any worries about money?

Push past the old "realistic" and "practical" limitations we've been giving our power away to our whole lives. Reach for the inner feeling of contentment and satisfaction that comes with tuning to a better future.

We can use this exercise for pretty much any thought that causes worry or doubt. The tricky part is recognizing when we're fixating on negative thoughts and stepping away from them and into this new game. It's not easy at first, but it is fun, and it can do wonders for our moods.

How great would it be to have plenty of support on our magical journey?

How great would it be to feel confident in all of our choices?

How great would it feel if life felt …great?

Posting little notes with reminders like "How great would it be if…" or "What a joy it will be when…" can be helpful when we're first trying to catch and stop our negative trains of thought.

This exercise addresses our negative thoughts that come from feeling stuck or powerless, it is not meant to be used to avoid our negative feelings. Negative feelings are the result of unmet needs; either here in our present reality or those rewired in our past, and should be processed with an appropriate shadow work technique, either solo or with someone who can help us meet our needs.

Exercise Six
Building Affirmations 2.0
Suggested -
Writing Sets of Affirmation: As needed
Repeating Sets of Affirmations: Daily (or as needed)

Affirmations are positive statements that we repeat to ourselves to remind ourselves of our best qualities and ultimate potential. A common approach to affirmations is the I AM statement, often repeated several times. However, the human brain is a fairly good lie detector, and repeated compliments we don't fully believe tend to set us off.

Try it.

Imagine a friend offers a compliment once.
It feels pretty good.

Now, imagine they repeat the exact same compliment. What happens to our warm fuzzy feelings? After a handful of repetitions, we may even feel a little anger creep in. We don't believe them anymore and, frankly, they're starting to irritate us. This is why affirmations don't always give us the instant, magical results we crave.

A more effective approach to affirmations is to design a progressive series of statements that acknowledge our natural or programmed reluctance to fully appreciating ourselves and gradually ease us from doubt to acceptance. We do this by adding two new types of statements before offering the affirmation; **forgiveness** and **anchoring**. Forgiveness statements give us the room necessary to accept and change any unwanted beliefs related to the area we're affirming. Forgiving ourselves and others is the way we clear our emotional space of debris before beginning the work of building a new foundation. Anchoring statements use our own positive memories, feelings and associations to prove that the things we are telling ourselves are true. By building with our very own memories, we can begin developing a foundation of trust to attach our affirmations to. This gives them the best opportunity to develop in our minds.

Forgiveness

Any "negative" belief can be addressed with targeted forgiveness.

"I forgive myself for believing that I can't do this and I now allow myself to do it anyway."

Whenever we notice negativity creeping in or resistance coming up we can go back into forgiveness mode and address anything that's coming up for us.

"I forgive myself for believing that unhealthy behaviors were acceptable and I now allow myself to change my views."

Remember, we don't have to forgive our past actions, only the beliefs that led us to take those actions.

"I forgive myself for believing I needed that and I now allow myself to change my thoughts."

Everyone has different phrases that work best for them, keep playing with ideas and changing up words until they feel right.

"It's OK that I believed that __(my heart's desire)__ was impossible, I'm ready to change my mind now."

As we begin to open up, discover, and write down our statements of forgiveness we're likely to stir up various inner voices. Though some moments may feel challenging, the overall effect should result in our feeling better and more confident as we progress. If we start to feel stuck or uncover something that feels unforgivable, we should probably consider talking about it with someone we trust.

It is healthy and freeing to forgive ourselves for not knowing any better in our past, allowing ourselves to move forward into a brighter future.

> **"I forgive myself for believing that
> I deserved to be unhappy
> and I now allow myself to smile."**

⚘ Anchoring

When our grumpy inner voices hear us forgiving ourselves, they'll often wake up to tell us that we're not being practical and we're going to fail - again. To help us defend ourselves against these old patterns of thought, we call on past experiences and anchor our new choices to old memories.

> **"I know how it feels to
> be in a healthy relationship
> because I really had fun
> hanging out with __(person)__ last week."**

This helps us to "prove" that we can be successful by reminding ourselves that we've been successful in the past. It may take a little creativity to outsmart and out-argue our inner critic, but our best tools for doing that are our emotional memories. Specifically, the ones that make us feel positive about whatever goal we're currently affirming

"I feel nurtured and satisfied when
I take the time to connect with my feelings
and meet my needs."

"It feels freeing and empowering
to stop worrying about relationships.
I trust myself to make healthy choices
for myself."

Choose an affirmation.

Write no more than 5 statements of forgiveness that support you where you feel weak on this topic. One effective format is "I forgive myself for ___ and now I allow myself to _____"

Write no more than 5 statements that anchor a positive emotional memory to past successes on this topic, "When __(specific related incident)__ happened, I felt __(positive feeling)__."

Follow these statements with your original affirmation and one or two more related affirmations.

Devote some time to reading and repeating the entire series of statements on a regular basis.

Exercise Six

Listen for any negative thoughts that show up and restart with forgiveness anytime old thoughts try to derail the process.

Keep updating and changing your statements to incorporate new experiences. Keep it fresh, the more you can really feel it the better.

Exercise Seven
Magick "To Do" Lists
Suggested - Weekly

This new twist on "To Do" lists allows more magick to enter our lives.

Draw a line dividing a sheet of paper into two equal halves.

Title one half "Things to do" and list the items you intend to do within the next few days to a week.

Title the other half "Things I will let magick do" and list all of the things that you choose not to spend the time, energy, money or worry on at this time.

Complete the tasks from your side of the list. Know that you need only do your part and simply trust that the items on the other side of the list are being handled.

When your to-do items are completed, make a new list. If an item from the magick side now sounds doable, move it to your list. Leave everything else just where it is and let the magick continue to work on them.

When choosing your tasks, only add things that feel fun, light, easy, desirable, or vitally important. Everything else; the complex, long-term and/or unpleasant tasks, should be delegated to the magick side until they feel more manageable.

By assigning specific responsibilities to the universe we can release ourselves from our own inner critic, giving us room to breathe. We are no longer ignoring our difficult tasks, we're delegating them to a higher power.

To be clear, this exercise isn't designed to create the miraculous, immediate completion of all of our undesirable and unpleasant tasks. It's designed to focus our energy on our highest priorities and let the rest go.

As we work through several rounds of this exercise, we often discover new insights, connections, or enthusiasm for tasks that we were stuck on before. Frequently we find several items are either taken care of for us or drop off of our lists, like magick.

Exercise Eight
Back From The Future Meditation
Suggested - At least once, repeat as desired

Have you ever imagined going back in time, visiting your younger self and giving them good advice? In this exercise, we flip that idea around and project ourselves forward into our ideal future. Meeting with our older self to explore future choices takes a little more focus and insight but with some imagination, we should be able to project our passions forward and dream as big as we possibly can.

[Begin with the connection technique in Exercise 2, then continue with…]

Feel the energy of your heart drawing you forward. You are moving into your future. From this moment, time speeds up in your life and you are making choices; what to eat, where to go, who to talk to. Hundreds of choices, every one of them leading to the perfect outcome for you. Over and over, you make choices and they lead you to the best possible result. Thousands of choices; what to study, what to create, what to care about. Millions of choices, years pass by in seconds and your streak of perfect choices continues. Everything goes your way. Now you are ten years into the future.

Exercise Eight

See yourself, ten years happier and more convinced than ever that life is absolutely amazing. This future version of you has seen ten years of opportunities and options go by. They are the result of the choices you made, the choices that made your life easier and brought you peace and serenity. This future you worries about nothing because they know that things always work out.

Spend some quality time asking questions and talking to your future self about their life.

Where do they live now? What do they create? Who are they closest to? What have they learned? Ask about the choices they made and the reasons why they made them. Take as much time as you like to get to know yourself.

When your conversation is over, offer your gratitude for this time and the insights it has given you and allow yourself to drift back to the present.

Write down any information you feel the need to.

Exercise Nine

Temple of Mind Meditation
Suggested - At least once, repeat as desired

The world can be an emotionally exhausting and brutal place. Most of us are living and working in spaces that don't feel sacred. We crave rest and relaxation but have difficulty finding it in our busy lives.

This exercise allows us to create and visit a sacred temple in our minds. Our internal sanctuary is a space for healing and peace. It is always available to us anywhere, and anywhen.

Most people find this meditation extremely enjoyable, but some do find themselves getting stuck, lost or afraid when working in this space. Acknowledge every feeling that comes up as valid and worthy, stopping the meditation if need be. Feel free to wait, change positions, take a walk, cry it out, phone a friend, take a nap, whatever feels most appealing before trying the meditation again. If the process causes overwhelming feelings of not being safe or spontaneous new memories of not feeling safe, please consider connecting with a trusted person who can effectively address emotional traumas.

[Begin with the connection technique in Exercise 2 then continue with…]

Exercise Nine

Something is pulling at the energy in your heart. A door appears in front of you. Only you can see this secret entrance, so only you can find it. There's nothing to be afraid of, your heart knows exactly where it's going. Open the door and step through.

As you do, notice that all of your stresses, worries, and anxieties are falling further and further behind you. They cannot follow you here. You feel that the door has closed behind you. In this space, there are no limits. Your sanctuary can be anything and everything that you need for it to be. It could be just like your favorite place on earth or something found only in myths and stories.

Look around. What can you see?

Listen. What can you hear?

What can you smell?

You discover your home somewhere in the sanctuary. It may be a tree house or a monastery, a cabin or a palace. Fill your home with the things that you love. As you do, you discover several safe places for you and your memories to lie down, rest and sleep.

Somewhere in your sanctuary, there's a water feature. A fountain, an ocean, a hot spring… whatever form it takes. The waters you find there have incredible healing powers. It doesn't even look like regular water; it's obviously very powerful, perfectly safe, liquid medicine for your physical, mental and energetic bodies. Go ahead and bathe in and drink this water to completely restore yourself.

You become aware of another being standing nearby and recognize them as a divine part of yourself. You feel their strength, their kindness, their devotion towards you and towards this temple.

This is your inner divinity. They maintain this sanctuary for you and their only desire is to keep you safe and help you grow stronger and more powerful. It may be a person or an angel, but it doesn't have to look human.

Greet them. Ask their name and any other questions you have. They will always be here for you in your safe haven. Spend some time getting to know your divine self.

Exercise Nine

Somewhere in your sanctuary is the safest place of all. A place where you can rest your body and completely relax. Outdoors or indoors, you are able to sink into the most peaceful and relaxing feeling you have ever experienced, your body feels completely supported, completely safe, totally relaxed.

You can return to this spot at any time you wish for a mini-vacation where you let everything go and just focus on the sounds, the smells, the textures, the beauty of the healing waters nearby. You are protected by the comforting presence of your divine self. Make it feel as real as you can for as long as you need to.

When you are ready to go, say goodbye to your divine self and assure them that you will take excellent care of yourself. Say goodbye to your temple and let it know you'll come back and visit soon. Feel yourself walking effortlessly toward the door that opens only for you. This door knows you and your unique way of opening the only gate into your safe haven. This door and the lock you set are absolutely secure in every way. No one else can ever come here unless you bring them in.

Take a few deep breaths and when you feel ready, open your eyes.

Once we've established a safe space for nurturing ourselves, we are free to spend as much time there as we like. Whenever we need a break from the daily world, we can visit our temple and recharge ourselves.

Exercise Ten
⇒⇐ Shadow Work Process ⇒⇐
Emotional Rewiring

Suggested - As needed

Shadow work is a broad term for any process that helps us sweep away the shadows that shroud our prism from the eternal flow of magick. Every "bad" feeling; our moments of depression, anxiety, anger, fear, jealousy, guilt, etc. is another opportunity to engage in shadow work.

Shadows are the result of our unresolved needs and the rewiring of our brains we chose in order to lessen our immediate sense of suffering. We did this long before we learned our language or understood complex human motivations, so these connections tend to be a little sloppy with shadows growing far out of proportion with the original, long forgotten issue. When these old connections are triggered we say that we behave "irrationally", yet we are acting in ways that seemed completely rational and reasonable to our younger self. This exercise can help us face our childhood shadows, rewire our emotions and restore the flow of magick through our lives.

Step One:

Complete the Temple of Mind meditation exercise number 9 before attempting the emotional rewiring process.

Shadow work is challenging, making it important to have a safe place to return to after exploring our memories, traumas, and spiritual wounds.

Please don't skip step one, OK?

Especially if it's difficult.

This exercise is based on a nearly universal belief that traumas can "fracture the soul" in some way. Different cultures explain the phenomenon in different ways but no matter how we imagine our shadows developing and hanging around, it's clear that all humans have them. This emotional rewiring process isn't the only way to address them but we strongly suggest using methods that result in the integration of our emotions instead of separating ourselves from them. Any process that suggests avoiding, cord cutting, or banishing memories, feelings, or people tends to result in more damage over time. This exercise depends on our powerful intention to embrace, explore, process, integrate and heal our uncomfortable feelings and emotions. Please see it as a framework to adjust according to your own experiences. Let it evolve for us as we work with it.

In practice, we begin by focusing our attention on some discomfort and moving through the following steps:

- Feel into the feeling
- Allow memories to surface and follow them
- Step into our story
- Retell the tale
- Call for fragments
- Bring everyone back to the temple
- Heal/Play/Resolve
- Integrate
- Appreciate
- Close the book

Exercise Ten

Address a current uncomfortable feeling or scan your body for feelings and sensations.

Stay with your feelings; allow them to command all of your attention. Declare that you are safe and it is normal to have strong feelings.

If a memory surfaces, allow yourself to go into it as deeply as possible, ideally remembering the scene as the child you were.

After reliving your memory, add your adult self as a new character in the scene. Ask your child self how to rewrite your memory and play through the new resolution in your mind. Repeat until your child self is satisfied with the outcome.

Call for any memory fragments to return to you and wait for them to do so. Repeat until you feel certain that all energy has returned.

Gather your child self and/or fragments and take them to your sanctuary from exercise nine. Allow your divine self to heal and restore both you and your retrieved sel(ves). Drink from your healing waters, share a meal of your favorite childhood foods, play, sing, rest.

Ask your retrieved self for consent to integrate before doing so.

Appreciate and thank yourself for your courage.

Close this chapter of your story and exit the visualization.

❧ Emotional Rewiring Process Details ❧

As we focus on our growth, we begin practicing an ongoing emotional awareness that eventually becomes second nature. We are learning to pay constant attention to what we are feeling, all the time, for the rest of our lives. If we start to feel "bad" and are unable to step into a better feeling, we can start seeing each discomfort as a tiny treasure giving us the potential for a deeper understanding of ourselves and our emotional landscape.

❧ Feel Into The Feeling

If we haven't practiced, it can be challenging to sit quietly embracing and appreciating our feelings instead of talking about them, acting on them, or letting them sweep us away. Sometimes we're struck by such strong feelings that we have to stop and embrace them. Either way, we begin by identifying the FEELING in the body. Not the words we call those feelings, or ways to "cure" them, just the physical feelings in our bodies right now.

"There's pressure in my throat. I can feel a weight on my shoulders. It's warm and I want to cry."

"My knee is tight, like a wound-up spring. There's kind of a dull throb running down my calf."

"My left eyebrow itches and there's a buzzing in my left ear."

Pay close attention to these feelings as they change and move around the body. It's critical to stay present and accept all of our feelings. Any sensation could be linked to significant emotions and a nurturing attitude is key.

"I feel an ache in my heart.
That's good, that's fine,
I'm OK.
I'm here with it.
Now my breath is slowing down,
it's harder to breathe.
It's all right.
I'm safe.
It's OK to feel this now."

Stopping to engage with our feelings may feel awkward and artificial at first, but it gets easier with practice, and the feelings that arise will become more obvious to us as we progress.

Follow The Memories

Sometimes feelings will bring up memories, often they don't. Some teachers believe that memory work is required, that we must relive our traumas to process them fully. We disagree.

A few of our memories may really want us to engage with them, but it's generally not necessary. A doctor doesn't need to know exactly how a bone was broken to set it back in place.

However, if a memory feels important, it usually is.

First check and make sure that you're focusing on the earliest memory you can find associated with your current feeling. Patterns tend to repeat in our lives and by engaging with the earliest event in the sequence we can often clear up the entire pattern.

Step Into The Story

Once we find our earliest associated memory, we relive it in as much detail as possible, through the eyes of our younger self. We're not trying to simply see the memory, we want to feel it again as much as possible. Pay close attention to the details, reminding yourself that you are safe now, safe enough to finally feel any pain you couldn't feel in the past and any pain you are still feeling today. Anything that feels right can help express our feelings (assuming we're not hurting ourselves or others); singing a song, throwing a pillow, letting the tears flow, howling at the moon…

If you don't experience a memory, stay with your feelings and ask yourself what would make them feel less overwhelming.

Retell The Tale

After getting deeply in touch with the memory or feeling we're working with, we can add a new character to our old story; our own adult self, our guardian angel, a fictional character, someone. It doesn't matter who it is as long as they genuinely love and care for us and that little version of us in the past.

Adding this hero self into the tale gives us the power to change our past, present and future right now. Tell a new tale that's as detailed and luxurious as possible. Be creative and do whatever soothes you.

We are here to slay our own personal dragons. We are free to tell ourselves epic tales of our superpowers, to wrap our tiny selves in blankets of calm, to vanquish any enemies, to reparent ourselves, to choose different thoughts, and grant ourselves the divine blessings of any number of deities and saints. Tell the story the way that it should have been told, tie up the loose ends, punish the bad guys, reward the heroes, nurture yourself in every conceivable way that you could possibly be nurtured. There are no limits here. Indeed, there's no benefit in rushing through this process as any work we leave undone will only pop up to be dealt with later on.

As we complete our new hero's tale, we ask ourselves at least twice how the tale should end, and answer without shame. Some fantasies may feel odd or disturbing but, as long as they remain imaginary, they can be powerfully healing as well.

Call For Fragments

When we call for the return of our lost, stuck, frozen or otherwise unavailable energy, we may feel bodily sensations or see things. There may be sounds, voices, or a sense of being joined by our younger self (selves).

We may have multiple memories to integrate so remain open and accepting of whatever comes, reassuring ourselves that it is safe to heal and we are ready to bring all our confused thoughts and fractured parts back to work together again.

> "It's safe. I'm safe.
> This feeling is coming from
> some other me in some other time.
> I love you. I'm here for you.
> It's safe now.
> Come join me."

The physical and emotional sensations of pulling ourselves back together can last for several minutes, so be patient and accepting as you wait for any and all fragments, shadows, soul chips or energy to return to you. This is no time for haste or coercion, we simply wait and integrate for as long as it takes until there is zero hesitation left and all of our inner voices are ready to move on.

Back To The Temple

Leaving no part of ourselves behind, we exit and delete the memory. Once cleared, we can head back to our safe haven where our divine self waits to nurture and tend to every single lost or wounded part of us.

Heal

We bathe in and drink from the healing waters. We play the games that we love. We spend as much time as we need making our past selves feel safe, whole, and loved. When we are finally ready, we can bring all of our selves, our divine self included, to the very safest spot in our temple and ask if we are ready to integrate.

~Integrate

If the answer is no, we can respect that and leave our separated selves to live and play in our sanctuary space until they feel whole enough to join us.

When the answer is yes, we can visualize all of our various parts fusing into the whole that is us. We restore our trapped energies, heal our splintered soul and identify ourselves as whole, complete and unified.

~Appreciate

Before closing, we offer thanks to our divine self, our past selves, and to our ordinary, everyday, amazing self.

Do not skip past the opportunity to appreciate yourself for actually doing this work. It isn't easy and not everyone will even attempt it, so recognize your efforts and give yourself some credit. OK?

~Close

No matter what happened during this exercise, it was exactly what it needed to be. Rewiring ourselves into our present is a continuous process that lasts a lifetime. This was merely one step in an endless journey, yet it was an extremely important one. Honor it as you feel led to and then let it be .

Come back to waking consciousness.

The next time you feel something come up, repeat the process.

You've got this!

☙ Pleasure Maps ❧

What brings you pleasure?

From our favorite pets to our favorite pet names to our favorite foods, fantasies and body parts, humans take pleasure in many different things. The pursuit of pleasure (happiness) is not merely a "right" but a highly effective way to enhance our vibration and improve our lives.

When creating maps to our own personal pleasures we should feel free to use photos, words, items, drawings, beloved artworks, etc.

Make it art. Make it you.

If you are so inspired, feel free to add more topics and pages to your map. Share your Pleasure Maps with supportive lovers, partners or companions, and ask them to complete one to share with you.

If something doesn't fit, feel free to skip it.

❧ Pleasure Map ☙

I am

_____

and you can call me

_____

or

_____

❧ Places ☙

I would like to live...

I would like to travel to...

❧ People ☙

I enjoy spending time with...

The qualities I most admire...

My role models are...

Pleasure Map

If I had three wishes I would...

One

Two

Three

Pleasure Map

My ideal life

My career

My car

My family

My home

My health

Pleasure Map

My favorite things

Styles

Pets/Animals

Music

Smells

Words

Foods

Books

Colors

Sounds

Pleasure Map

My greatest acomplishments are...

I'd like to learn to...

My personal mottos are...

Pleasure Map

My favorite things about my body are...

My favorite intimate experience was...

I would like to try...

Pleasure Map

I like it when my lovers...

I don't like it when my lovers...

I feel amazing when I...

ॐ Appreciation Journal ॐ

Gratitude tends to come with a small side of unworthiness, courtesy of humanity's long history with God, so we focus on the feeling of appreciation which has a higher vibration without the undertone of fear.

An appreciation journal is a place to write about the things we appreciate. Some entries are stream of consciousness exercises focusing on a single facet of our lives; our partner, a new project, holiday plans, etc. The page here offers a little structure for days when we need prompts to help us remember the things we encountered throughout our day.

Copy this sample page, modify it, punch holes in the pages and add it to a binder. It makes for a unique, personalized appreciation journal.

When we focus on how amazing things already are, life gets easier.

Enjoy!

Appreciation Journal

Date
_____

I appreciate...

The best part of the day was...

I really liked it when...

I laughed at...

I'd like more of...

ᴆ Kya's Story ᴂ

When I was little, I had a book of children's Bible stories along with my Grimm's tales, my 1001 Arabian Nights, the entire series of Oz books and a collection of Greek myths. It took me a while to realize that some people took the one book far more seriously than the others.

Answering a classified ad in the back of Rolling Stone magazine, I enrolled in the School of Wicca correspondence course at the age of 16. As I made my way through the eclectic reading list, my independent spiritual education began. I read anthropology, biology, various holy books, science journals, essays on religion, and a steady stream of spiritual and New Age thought. I admired various indigenous spiritual traditions but never overcame my consumerism-based worldview; so I became just another spiritual eclectic. A white, female, "New Age" solitary dabbler in faith with no real traditions to guide or ground her.

At 24, I became a mother and soon had my first "atheist" awakening. Holding my newborn daughter, Faerin, in my arms, I realized I would always forgive her. There was nothing she could possibly do, no crime she could ever commit, that I wouldn't forgive her for. I fully rejected the idea of any God that could leave even a single one of his beloved children to eternal punishment. My heart was telling me, "That's not how love, or parenting, works."

Despite my rejection of a judgmental God, I really didn't consider myself an atheist. I continued to believe in a universe that loved and supported me. I couldn't have explained the exact nature of this relationship, but I remained in the "I believe in something I call God" camp until 2005 when my life changed virtually overnight, leaving me an unsupported, unemployed, single mother homeschooling three young children.

Life as a single mother wasn't easy. Our lives got hard and my heart began to harden as well. In time, our little family of four managed to produce three self-avowed atheists. My youngest son still truly wanted to believe, but his tender faith wasn't able to withstand our constant rational questioning. I was absolutely confident in my assertions that there was no God, no compassionate creator, no supportive universe, just a cold emotionless reality that didn't care about me or my children at all.

Life as an atheist really wasn't all that bad. I didn't "hate" or "resent" God, I just didn't believe in it anymore. I believed that I was entirely on my own, but I homeschooled the kids, got a job, bought a house, sent the kids to college. We actually did fairly well.

Until we didn't.

On May 19, 2015, Faerin ended her own life. She hid her symptoms of depression from me, from her friends, and her therapist. She surprised us all. My inner world shattered in an afternoon and I was left to pick up whatever pieces of my life and my identity I could still find.

Everything I thought I knew was suddenly called into question; especially my atheism, God, religion, life, death, and the true purpose of humanity. I was actively haunted by Faerin's favorite (if frequently flippant) question, "Why is life so hard?"

As I struggled with my new reality, I began a journey to find my purpose and realized just how powerful the forces of both theism and atheism had been in my life. Despite the wisdom of both philosophies, they each only present us with a small part of the bigger spiritual truth. The conflicts between the facts and the fictions had left me confused and weary. Without a more honest, balanced view of reality, I was doomed to living only half a life, ultimately damaging myself, my relationships, my family and my community. When I began to realize this, I suddenly saw clearly that, as far as I could tell, our entire culture was suffering from some form of this spiritual confusion.

Lost and facing the pain of spending the rest of my life without my precious child, I asked a new, desperate version of her favorite question, "Hey God, why is life so hard?"

Unexpectedly, shockingly, against all odds, I got an answer. It wasn't an easy answer or a quick answer. It wasn't an answer that my skeptical, atheist mind wanted to accept, because it wasn't entirely rational or measurable, but I'm living according to the answer and life isn't as hard now. In fact, it's kind of fun and it's getting better by the day.

Hey God, Why Is Life So Hard?

Notes

Notes

ꙮ About the Author ꙮ

Kya Rose was the atheist mother of three until the unexpected suicide of her only daughter caused her to question everything. An ordained Humanist minister and Reiki master teacher, as well as the former webmistress of EmpoweredChildbirth.com, Kya has been speaking and writing about feminism, human rights, culture, and health for decades.

Kya's passion is for reconnecting folks to the divinity within them. She says she's on a mission to "give God back to the people".

This is her first book.

www.ingramcontent.com/pod-product-compliance
Lightning Source LLC
Chambersburg PA
CBHW031123080526
44587CB00011B/1092